GO
AND FIND
A DONKEY

MULTIPLE CHOICE BIBLE STUDIES FOR HOLY WEEK

CELESTA LETCHWORTH

Fermata House
www.fermatahouse.com

ISBN: 978-1-947566-02-6
Library of Congress Control Number: 2019903339

Published by Fermata House: Versailles, Kentucky www.fermatahouse.com

Unless otherwise noted, Scripture quotations are taken from the Holy Bible: World English Bible. The World English Bible (WEB) is a Public Domain Modern English translation of the Holy Bible. The World English Bible is based on the American Standard Version of the Holy Bible first published in 1901, the Biblia Hebraica Stutgartensa Old Testament, and the Greek Majority Text New Testament.

Cover and chapter title fonts:
   Optimus Princeps by Manfred Klein.

Cover photo:
   20120106-OC-AMW-0238 by the U.S. Department of Agriculture, is in the public domain. Original and mirror images cropped.
   Description: *A female donkey and her foal graze on a farm in Delaware on July 7, 2008. A male donkey or ass is called a jack, a female a jenny or jennet. USDA photo by Alice Welch.*

FROM THE
CHOOSE THIS DAY

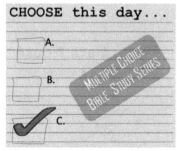

MULTIPLE
CHOICE
BIBLE
STUDY
SERIES

I am especially grateful for the folks who tested these Holy Week Bible Studies at St. James, Salem, and Marion United Methodist Churches.

Join the Team

You can help improve the *Choose This Day Multiple Choice Bible Study Series* by sending your **comments** to www.fermatahouse.com/contact.

And you can help make the Series more accessible to others by leaving a **review** on amazon.com. Amazon's search engine has an algorithm for visibility which is largely based on the number of **reviews** a book receives. Just a few words will suffice.

Thanks in advance!

CONTENTS

INTRODUCTION

Go and find a donkey. That's what Jesus said to two of his disciples. The Gospel of Matthew spends seven verses describing the logistics of acquiring a donkey. Mark and Luke do the same. Holy week begins with the donkey.

On Palm Sunday, we celebrate the Triumphal Entry of Jesus into Jerusalem, riding the donkey. The crowd waves palm branches and shouts, "Hosanna!" But Matthew, Mark, and Luke only spend two or three verses describing this parade. That's less than half of the verses devoted to acquiring the donkey.

Donkeys must be important.

The disciples found the donkey and her colt in the village, just as Jesus described. They were in the right place at the right time and were available to be used by our Lord. *Am I willing and making myself available to be used by our Lord?*

In the first chapter of this book, you'll read about how Jesus fulfilled Zechariah's prophecy when he rode the donkey into Jerusalem. Warfaring kings rode horses. Peaceful kings rode donkeys. Donkeys represent humility and peace. *Does my life represent humility and peace?*

I find donkeys fascinating. Did you know that the reason they're stubborn is because they have a strong sense of self-preservation? They're just being cautious. Isn't it interesting that the Gospel writers never mention a stubborn donkey. Evidently, the donkey trusted Jesus and felt safe wherever Jesus led it. *Oh, that I might trust Jesus wherever he leads me. May I live in the assurance of his security so that I don't respond with stubbornness.*

But this book isn't about donkeys. This book is about the last week that Jesus spent on Earth as the Son of Man — the week that we call *Holy Week*. Starting on Palm Sunday and ending on Easter Monday, we'll be studying these events as they are recorded in the Gospel of Matthew.

Use these studies personally during a coffee break or with your family in the car or at the breakfast table. They're short. They're fun. They're easy. Use them on the suggested dates, or skip around. Use your own Bible to read the Scripture passages or read them as they're printed in each chapter (from the World English Bible translation).

No need to feel intimidated if you're not familiar with some of these Scriptures — the answers to the multiple choice questions are in the back of the book. Those who have test-driven these Bible studies range from seminary graduates to those who are new to the faith.

As we enter Holy Week, I pray that this Bible study will help you be like the donkey that was there on Day One. As God's servants, we must:

- Be willing and available to be used by God.
- Represent humility and peace in a world that empha-sizes an ego-centric, selfish culture.
- Not be stubborn, but be able to feel the assurance that we can safely go wherever God leads us.

FAQ

How long will this study take?

Each day's Bible study should take 10–15 minutes. If you wish to spend more time each day, you could re-read the entire Scripture passage when you're finished, reflecting on your new-found understanding. If you're doing this Holy Week Bible Study with someone else, you could use the Meditation section as a discussion starter.

How many days will this Bible study last?

The Holy Week Bible Study lasts for nine days, starting on Palm Sunday and ending on Easter Monday.

Can I do each day's study by myself, or is this just for families?

You can certainly do the Holy Week Bible Study by yourself. In fact, you could squeeze it in during a coffee break or at bedtime. But why not make a covenant with another person to do this study together? You could meet in person or over the phone.

Do you have any suggestions about how to use the Holy Week Bible Study effectively?

The directions for each day's study include — read the entire Scripture passage first. Then **re-read each section BEFORE** answering the questions. This way you will get more out of the Scripture reading. It will also improve listening skills for those around the table.

How do I know when I answer a question correctly or incorrectly?
Each question is answered in the Scripture passage immediately preceding it. Some answers paraphrase the actual Scripture, but in those cases, the correct answers are designed to be more obvious. And you can always check out the list of answers in the back of the book.

Do I _have_ to re-read the verses before answering the questions?
Yes, please. This Bible study is designed so that each day you will have read the selected Scripture passage three times — first the entire passage, then a smaller section, then re-read the smaller section to double-check your answers.

Can I use my own Bible to read each day's Scripture passages?
Sure. The verses are printed as part of each day's study, but you can read them from your own Bible instead. Just be aware that some translations use different spellings/pronunciations of people's names. For example, some translations of Matthew 27:56 mention Mary the mother of James and _Joses_. Other translations list her as Mary the mother of James and _Joseph_. (The Greek word, _Joses_, is a variant of _Joseph_.)

You'll also run into minor semantics like in Matthew 27:26 when the word _flog_ is used in some translations, while other translations describe Jesus' torture as _scourge_ and _severely whipped_.

I can't start on Palm Sunday. Should I wait until next year?
You can jump in anytime you want, or you can disregard the dates and use this book as nine Bible studies that cover the last week of Jesus' life on Earth as recorded in the Gospel of Matthew. You can also skip around and not do them in chronological order.

Are there more Bible studies like this?
Fermata House released _Getting Ready for Christmas: 25 Multiple Choice Bible Studies for Advent_ in November, 2018. It is available in print and Kindle formats at Amazon.

More studies are being developed as part of the *Choose This Day Multiple Choice Bible Study Series*, including parables and miracles; the book of James, Psalms, and a look at the faith folks listed in the eleventh chapter of Hebrews.

Your suggestions and feedback are invaluable!

Please reach out through www.fermatahouse.com/contact.

Palm Sunday

First read the entire passage — Matthew 21:1–14.

When they came near to Jerusalem, and came to Bethsphage, to the Mount of Olives, then Jesus sent two disciples, saying to them, "Go into the village that is opposite you, and immediately you will find a donkey tied, and a colt with her. Untie them, and bring them to me. If anyone says anything to you, you shall say, 'The Lord needs them,' and immediately he will send them."

All this was done, that it might be fulfilled which was spoken through the prophet, saying,
"Tell the daughter of Zion, behold, your King comes to you, humble, and riding on a donkey, on a colt, the foal of a donkey."

The disciples went, and did just as Jesus commanded them, and brought the donkey and the colt, and laid their clothes on them; and he sat on them. A very great multitude spread their clothes on the road. Others cut branches from the trees, and spread them on the road. The multitudes who went in front of him, and those who followed, kept shouting, "Hosanna to the son of David! Blessed is he who comes in the name of the Lord! Hosanna in the highest!"
When he had come into Jerusalem, all the city was stirred up, saying, "Who is this?" The multitudes said, "This is the prophet, Jesus, from Nazareth of Galilee."

Jesus entered into the temple of God, and drove out all of those who sold and bought in the temple, and overthrew the money changers' tables and the seats of those who sold the doves. He said to them, "It is written, 'My house shall be called a house of prayer,' but you have made it a den of robbers!" The blind and the lame came to him in the temple, and he healed them.

Now re-read verses 1–3.

> When they came near to Jerusalem, and came to Bethsphage, to the Mount of Olives, then Jesus sent two disciples, saying to them, "Go into the village that is opposite you, and immediately you will find a donkey tied, and a colt with her. Untie them, and bring them to me. If anyone says anything to you, you shall say, 'The Lord needs them,' and immediately he will send them."

1. Where are Jesus and his disciples?
   a) Just outside Shemar, at Mt. Gerizim.
   b) Just outside Jerusalem, at the Mount of Olives.
   c) Just outside Philadelphia, at Valley Forge National Park.

2. Jesus sends somebody to do an errand for him. Who does he send?
   a) Two of his disciples.
   b) Two blind men that he just healed in Matthew 20:30–34.
   c) Superman and Lois Lane.

3. Where does Jesus send them?
   a) To the garden of Gethsemane.
   b) To the village of Bethsphage.
   c) To the town of Bethlehem.

4. Jesus tells them they'll find two things just inside the village. What are they?
   a) A garden and a place to pray.
   b) A donkey and its baby.
   c) A manger and a baby.

5. When they pick up these two things, what are they to do if anyone asks them what they're doing?
   a) They're to put them back where they found them.
   b) They're to run away.
   c) They're to say, "The Lord needs them."

In verse 5, Matthew quotes the prophet Zechariah from the Old Testament. Read Zechariah 9:9.

> Rejoice greatly, daughter of Zion! Shout, daughter of Jerusalem! Behold, your King comes to you! He is righteous, and having salvation; lowly, and riding on a donkey, even on a colt, the foal of a donkey.

Now re-read verses 4–5.

> All this was done, that it might be fulfilled which was spoken through the prophet, saying,
> "Tell the daughter of Zion, behold, your King comes to you, humble, and riding on a donkey, on a colt, the foal of a donkey."

1. Why did Jesus tell them to go to the village and bring back a donkey and her colt?
   a. So he could fulfill the prophecy.
   b. So he could add to his collection of rescued farm animals.
   c. So he could take a nap while they were in the village.

2. According to the prophecy, the humble King arrives, riding on a
   a. Horse
   b. Donkey
   c. Skateboard

3. Zechariah's prophecy is about the King of Israel. Who do you think is the king that fulfills this prophecy?
   a. Jesus
   b. John the Baptist
   c. Henry VIII

Now re-read verses 6–11.

"Hosanna" is a Hebrew word which loosely translated means "Save Us!"

> The disciples went, and did just as Jesus commanded them, and brought the donkey and the colt, and laid their clothes on them; and he sat on them. A very great multitude spread their clothes on the road. Others cut branches from the trees, and spread them on the

> road. The multitudes who went in front of him, and those who followed, kept shouting, "Hosanna to the son of David! Blessed is he who comes in the name of the Lord! Hosanna in the highest!" When he had come into Jerusalem, all the city was stirred up, saying, "Who is this?" The multitudes said, "This is the prophet, Jesus, from Nazareth of Galilee."

1. What did some people in the crowd do when they saw Jesus riding into Jerusalem?
    a) They spread their coats and tree branches on the road before him.
    b) They grabbed Jesus and put him in jail.
    c) They looked the other way.

2. What did the crowd say?
    a) They insulted Jesus and his disciples.
    b) They shouted praises to Jesus.
    c) They begged Jesus to heal them.

Now re-read verses 12–14.

> Jesus entered into the temple of God, and drove out all of those who sold and bought in the temple, and overthrew the money changers' tables and the seats of those who sold the doves. He said to them, "It is written, 'My house shall be called a house of prayer,' but you have made it a den of robbers!" The blind and the lame came to him in the temple, and he healed them.

1. Here Matthew changes scenes. Where is Jesus now?
    a) In the temple.
    b) In jail.
    c) In Hollywood, helping make the movie, *Ben Hur*.

2. Why does Jesus drive out the merchants?
    a) Because they made fun of him.
    b) Because God's house is for prayer.
    c) Because there is a bomb threat, so it is too dangerous for them to stay.

3. What did Jesus do when the sick people came up to him?
    a) He drove them out too.
    b) He told them to sacrifice a pigeon or dove to the Lord.
    c) He healed them.

MEDITATION:

When Jesus sent his two disciples on an errand to find the donkey and her colt, they may have thought it was a menial, unimportant task.

God has many errands for us. Some tasks seem small and simple; some tasks seem great and more complicated. None are more important than others. Our job is only to obey gladly.

What are some of the errands God is asking you to do today?

What are some of the errands God is asking you to do this month?

What are some of the errands God is asking you to do this year?

Holy Monday

First read the entire passage — Matthew 26:1–16.

When Jesus had finished all these words, he said to his disciples, "You know that after two days the Passover is coming, and the Son of Man will be delivered up to be crucified."

Then the chief priests, the scribes, and the elders of the people were gathered together in the court of the high priest, who was called Caiaphas. They took counsel together that they might take Jesus by deceit, and kill him. But they said, "Not during the feast, lest a riot occur among the people."

Now when Jesus was in Bethany, in the house of Simon the leper, a woman came to him having an alabaster jar of very expensive ointment, and she poured it on his head as he sat at the table. But when his disciples saw this, they were indignant, saying, "Why this waste? For this ointment might have been sold for much, and given to the poor."
However, knowing this, Jesus said to them, "Why do you trouble the woman? Because she has done a good work for me. For you always have the poor with you; but you don't always have me. For in pouring this ointment on my body, she did it to prepare me for burial. Most certainly I tell you, wherever this Good News is preached in the whole world, what this woman has done will also be spoken of as a memorial of her."

Then one of the twelve, who was called Judas Iscariot, went to the chief priests, and said, "What are you willing to give me, that I should deliver him to you?" They weighed out for him thirty pieces of silver. From that time he sought opportunity to betray him.

Now re-read verses 1–2.

> When Jesus had finished all these words, he said to his disciples, "You know that after two days the Passover is coming, and the Son of Man will be delivered up to be crucified."

1. Who is Jesus talking to here?
   a) His disciples.
   b) The chief priests.
   c) His mother, Mary.

2. Jesus says that a certain Jewish holiday is coming in two days. What is it?
   a) Easter
   b) Fourth of July.
   c) Passover.

3. Jesus is prophesying that something will happen to the Son of Man during this holiday. What is it?
   a) He will be killed.
   b) He will take over the Roman government.
   c) He will be the star of a Reality TV show.

4. Who do you think the *Son of Man* is?
   a) Jesus
   b) Jesus' mother, Mary
   c) Huckleberry Finn

Jesus refers to himself as the Son of Man 30 times in the Gospel of Matthew. When the first Christian martyr, Stephen, was stoned to death, his last words were: *Behold, I see the heavens opened, and the Son of Man standing at the right hand of God!* (Acts 7:56)

Now re-read verses 3–5.

> Then the chief priests, the scribes, and the elders of the people were gathered together in the court of the high priest, who was called Caiaphas. They took counsel together that they might take Jesus by

deceit, and kill him. But they said, "Not during the feast, lest a riot occur among the people."

1. Meanwhile, some people are plotting to kill Jesus. Who are they?
   a) The chief priests and other religious leaders.
   b) Darth Vader and his stormtroopers.
   c) Jesus' disciples.

2. Where are these people meeting?
   a) At the home of Simon, a leper.
   b) At the home of Caiaphas, a chief priest.
   c) At the home of Herod, the king.

3. They decide to kill Jesus, but not during the Passover celebration. Why not during Passover?
   a) No one can be arrested during Passover.
   b) There are a lot of people in the city during Passover, and they might cause a riot.
   c) It's against the law to kill anyone during Passover.

Now re-read verses 6–13.

Now when Jesus was in Bethany, in the house of Simon the leper, a woman came to him having an alabaster jar of very expensive ointment, and she poured it on his head as he sat at the table. But when his disciples saw this, they were indignant, saying, "Why this waste? For this ointment might have been sold for much, and given to the poor."

However, knowing this, Jesus said to them, "Why do you trouble the woman? Because she has done a good work for me. For you always have the poor with you; but you don't always have me. For in pouring this ointment on my body, she did it to prepare me for burial. Most certainly I tell you, wherever this Good News is preached in the whole world, what this woman has done will also be spoken of as a memorial of her."

1. Now Jesus is in Bethany, eating. What happens?
   a) He feeds everyone with just two fish and five loaves of bread.
   b) He heals a leper.
   c) A lady pours perfume on his head.

2. Why are the disciples upset when this happens?
   a) They don't want to clean up the mess.
   b) They think it's a waste of good money.
   c) They're mad because they didn't think of it first.

3. What does Jesus say about all this?
   a) "Throw this woman out of here!"
   b) "This woman did a good thing."
   c) "Will this stuff wash out?"

4. Jesus says that this act symbolizes his preparation for something. What is it?
   a) His shampoo, cut, and style.
   b) His crowning as the new king.
   c) His burial.

Now re-read verses 14–16

> Then one of the twelve, who was called Judas Iscariot, went to the chief priests, and said, "What are you willing to give me, that I should deliver him to you?" They weighed out for him thirty pieces of silver. From that time he sought opportunity to betray him.

1. Which one of the twelve apostles (or, main disciples) meets with the chief priests?
   a) Judas Iscariot
   b) Simon the Zealot
   c) Simon Peter

2. He makes a deal with the chief priests. What kind of deal is it?
   a) He will sing at their next worship service if they get him a good accompanist.
   b) He will give them all the apostles' money if they promise to protect them from the Romans.
   c) He will deliver Jesus into their hands if they pay him.

MEDITATION:

When the woman anoints Jesus with expensive perfume, the disciples are upset about the waste of money. All they can see at this time are the dollars and cents.

But what Jesus is concerned with is the woman's motive for this action. Her motive is love.

What would you do for Jesus today without counting the cost?

Here are a couple of examples to help you start thinking of what you could do:

- Skipping a TV show to read the Bible.

- Giving half of your sandwich to someone who has nothing to eat.

- Donating your time and/or money to an organization that helps people.

Holy Tuesday

First read the entire passage — Matthew 26: 17–30.

Now on the first day of unleavened bread, the disciples came to Jesus, saying to him, "Where do you want us to prepare for you to eat the Passover?"

He said, "Go into the city to a certain person, and tell him, 'The Teacher says, "My time is at hand. I will keep the Passover at your house with my disciples.""''

The disciples did as Jesus commanded them, and they prepared the Passover. Now when evening had come, he was reclining at the table with the twelve disciples. As they were eating, he said, "Most certainly I tell you that one of you will betray me."

They were exceedingly sorrowful, and each began to ask him, "It isn't me, is it, Lord?"

He answered, "He who dipped his hand with me in the dish, the same will betray me. The Son of Man goes, even as it is written of him, but woe to that man through whom the Son of Man is betrayed! It would be better for that man if he had not been born." Judas, who betrayed him, answered, "It isn't me, is it, Rabbi?"

He said to him, "You said it."

As they were eating, Jesus took bread, gave thanks for it, and broke it. He gave to the disciples, and said, "Take, eat; this is my body."

He took the cup, gave thanks, and gave to them, saying, "All of you drink it, for this is my blood of the new covenant, which is poured out for many for the remission of sins. But I tell you that I will not drink of this fruit of the vine from now on, until that day when I drink it anew with you in my Father's Kingdom." When they had sung a hymn, they went out to the Mount of Olives.

Now re-read verses 17–22.

> Now on the first day of unleavened bread, the disciples came to Jesus, saying to him, "Where do you want us to prepare for you to eat the Passover?"
> He said, "Go into the city to a certain person, and tell him, 'The Teacher says, "My time is at hand. I will keep the Passover at your house with my disciples."'"
> The disciples did as Jesus commanded them, and they prepared the Passover. Now when evening had come, he was reclining at the table with the twelve disciples. As they were eating, he said, "Most certainly I tell you that one of you will betray me."
> They were exceedingly sorrowful, and each began to ask him, "It isn't me, is it, Lord?"

1. The disciples ask Jesus where he wants to eat a certain meal. What is that meal?
   a) Christmas meal.
   b) Passover meal.
   c) Easter meal.

2. With whom does Jesus eat the Passover meal?
   a) The chief priests and elders.
   b) The ten cleansed lepers.
   c) His twelve disciples.

3. Jesus tells them that one of them will betray him. How does this make them feel?
   a) They are sad.
   b) They are excited.
   c) They are thankful.

4. What do each of the disciples ask Jesus?
   a) "Where did you get such a silly idea?"
   b) "Is Judas the one who will betray you?"
   c) "Am I the one who will betray you?"

Now re-read verses 23–25.

Here's some notes to help you understand verses 23–25 better:

The **dish** Jesus refers to is a bowl that has **charoset** sauce in it. At a certain point in the Passover meal, each person dips bitter herbs in the charoset and then eats them.

It's interesting that Jesus refers to this bitter symbolic part of the Passover meal when He speaks of the betrayal.

> He answered, "He who dipped his hand with me in the dish, the same will betray me. The Son of Man goes, even as it is written of him, but woe to that man through whom the Son of Man is betrayed! It would be better for that man if he had not been born." Judas, who betrayed him, answered, "It isn't me, is it, Rabbi?" He said to him, "You said it."

1. What does Jesus say about the one who will betray him?
    a) He will be crucified with Jesus.
    b) He will receive his reward in Heaven.
    c) He'd be better off if he'd never been born.

2. When a certain disciple asks Jesus if he is the one who will betray him, Jesus says he is. Who is this disciple?
    a) Peter
    b) Judas
    c) Andrew

Now re-read verse 26.

> As they were eating, Jesus took bread, gave thanks for it, and broke it. He gave to the disciples, and said, "Take, eat; this is my body."

1. Jesus picks up some bread which is not part of the Passover tradition. What does he do before he breaks the bread?
    a) He checks the sides and bottom of the bread for mold.
    b) He asks the host if they have jelly for the bread.
    c) He gives thanks for the bread with a blessing.

2. What does Jesus say when he breaks the bread that is not part of the Passover tradition?
   a) "This is my body."
   b) "This is my blood."
   c) "This is the bread."

Now re-read verses 27-30

> He took the cup, gave thanks, and gave to them, saying, "All of you drink it, for this is my blood of the new covenant, which is poured out for many for the remission of sins. But I tell you that I will not drink of this fruit of the vine from now on, until that day when I drink it anew with you in my Father's Kingdom." When they had sung a hymn, they went out to the Mount of Olives.

1. What does Jesus do after he picks up the cup?
   a) He takes a sip to test it.
   b) He gives thanks for it.
   c) He admires the design and asks his host where he bought it.

2. When Jesus passes the cup, what does he say that it is?
   a) Jesus' blood of the new covenant.
   b) Jesus' blood of the ten commandments.
   c) Jesus' blood of the parables.

3. Jesus' blood makes it possible for what?
   a) For many to come to church and worship freely.
   b) For many to be forgiven of their sins.
   c) For many to have lots of money and be famous.

4. What do they do after the Passover meal?
   a) They sing a hymn and then walk to the Mount of Olives.
   b) They play ping-pong and then have dessert.
   c) They study the Bible and then walk to Gethsemane.

MEDITATION:

When Jesus says that one of the disciples will betray him, each of the disciples looks into his own heart and asks the question, "Is it I?" They realize that, in certain situations, they might be weak enough to betray Jesus.

Some of the ways we betray Jesus are:

- To disappoint him by sinning against him.

- To behave in a way that is not Christlike.

- To refuse to help someone in need.

When was the last time you betrayed Jesus?

Take time now to ask Jesus to forgive you and to help you prevent this from happening again. Perhaps he will inspire you with a practical solution, or maybe he will inspire you with a feeling of his love and strength.

Spy Wednesday

First read the entire passage — Matthew 26:36–50.

Then Jesus came with them to a place called Gethsemane, and said to his disciples, "Sit here, while I go there and pray." He took with him Peter and the two sons of Zebedee, and began to be sorrowful and severely troubled. Then he said to them, "My soul is exceedingly sorrowful, even to death. Stay here, and watch with me."

He went forward a little, fell on his face, and prayed, saying, "My Father, if it is possible, let this cup pass away from me; nevertheless, not what I desire, but what you desire."

He came to the disciples, and found them sleeping, and said to Peter, "What, couldn't you watch with me for one hour? Watch and pray, that you don't enter into temptation. The spirit indeed is willing, but the flesh is weak."

Again, a second time he went away, and prayed, saying, "My Father, if this cup can't pass away from me unless I drink it, your desire be done." He came again and found them sleeping, for their eyes were heavy. He left them again, went away, and prayed a third time, saying the same words. Then he came to his disciples, and said to them, "Sleep on now, and take your rest. Behold, the hour is at hand, and the Son of Man is betrayed into the hands of sinners. Arise, let's be going. Behold, he who betrays me is at hand."

While he was still speaking, behold, Judas, one of the twelve, came, and with him a great multitude with swords and clubs, from the chief priest and elders of the people. Now he who betrayed him gave them a sign, saying, "Whoever I kiss, he is the one. Seize him." Immediately he came to Jesus, and said, "Hail, Rabbi!" and kissed him. Jesus said to him, "Friend, why are you here?" Then they came and laid hands on Jesus, and took him.

Now re-read verses 36–38.

Then Jesus came with them to a place called Gethsemane, and said to his disciples, "Sit here, while I go there and pray." He took with him Peter and the two sons of Zebedee, and began to be sorrowful and severely troubled. Then he said to them, "My soul is exceedingly sorrowful, even to death. Stay here, and watch with me."

1. Where do Jesus and his disciples go?
   a) Jerusalem
   b) Nazareth
   c) Gethsemane

2. When Jesus goes over there to pray, who does he take with him?
   a) Judas Iscariot and Judas the son of James.
   b) Peter and the two Zebedee brothers.
   c) Peter and Philip and Thomas.

3. Jesus tells them how he feels. What does he say to them?
   a) I am SO sad.
   b) I'm looking forward to being king.
   c) Let's go to Galilee and preach to the people.

4. What does he tell them to do?
   a) Lie here and rest.
   b) Go and get food for us to eat.
   c) Stay awake with me.

Now re-read verse 39.

He went forward a little, fell on his face, and prayed, saying, "My Father, if it is possible, let this cup pass away from me; nevertheless, not what I desire, but what you desire."

1. Jesus then walks a few steps away from them and prays to God. In the first half of his prayer, what does he ask God to do?
   a) Father, help me conquer the Romans.
   b) Father, take this cup from me.
   c) Father, I'm thirsty. Give me something to drink.

2. "Let this cup pass from me" is a figure of speech. What do you think Jesus means?
   a) I'm really not thirsty now.
   b) I don't want to preach anymore.
   c) I really don't want to be crucified.

3. How does Jesus end his prayer to God?
   a) Go ahead and do what You want with me.
   b) In the name of the Father and the Son and the Holy Spirit, amen.
   c) For Thine is the kingdom and the power, and the glory forever and ever.

Now re-read verses 40–41.

> He came to the disciples, and found them sleeping, and said to Peter, "What, couldn't you watch with me for one hour? Watch and pray, that you don't enter into temptation. The spirit indeed is willing, but the flesh is weak."

1. Meanwhile, what are the three disciples doing?
   a) Running away.
   b) Eating the olives in the garden.
   c) Sleeping.

2. How does Jesus feel about their action?
   a) He is disappointed.
   b) He is pleased.
   c) He is apathetic (doesn't care).

3. Jesus tells them to stay awake and pray. Why should they stay awake and pray?
   a) So they will be able to help Jesus fight the Romans.
   b) So they will be in shape for their church's Walkathon the next day.
   c) So they won't give in to temptation.

4. Jesus tells them that, "the spirit is willing, but the flesh is weak." What do you think he means?
   a) They have good intentions, but it's hard for them to carry them out.
   b) They like sports, but they're not very good athletes.
   c) He wants them to go on a diet, but they keep eating everything in sight.

Now re-read verses 42–46.

> Again, a second time he went away, and prayed, saying, "My Father, if this cup can't pass away from me unless I drink it, your desire be done." He came again and found them sleeping, for their eyes were heavy. He left them again, went away, and prayed a third time, saying the same words. Then he came to his disciples, and said to them, "Sleep on now, and take your rest. Behold, the hour is at hand, and the Son of Man is betrayed into the hands of sinners. Arise, let's be going. Behold, he who betrays me is at hand."

1. How many times does Jesus pray?
   a) 3
   b) 1
   c) 5

2. After he finishes praying, Jesus tells them that now is the time for something to happen to the Son of Man. What is that something?
   a) It's time for him to get married.
   b) He is being nominated for the "Son of the Year" award.
   c) Someone is betraying him.

Now re-read verses 47–50.

> While he was still speaking, behold, Judas, one of the twelve, came, and with him a great multitude with swords and clubs, from the chief priest and elders of the people. Now he who betrayed him gave them a sign, saying, "Whoever I kiss, he is the one. Seize him." Immediately he came to Jesus, and said, "Hail, Rabbi!" and kissed him. Jesus said to him, "Friend, why are you here?" Then they came and laid hands on Jesus, and took him.

1. Who comes to Jesus?
    a) Judas Iscariot and a crowd of people.
    b) King Herod and Pontius Pilate.
    c) Jesus' mother, Mary.

2. In those days, people kissed each other on the cheek as a way of greeting each other. This is similar to the 21st century American greeting of shaking hands. Why does Judas kiss Jesus?
    a) To show Jesus that he loves him and he's sorry for what he has done.
    b) To identify Jesus to the crowd as the man they should arrest.
    c) To congratulate Jesus for receiving the Humanitarian of the Year award.

3. What does the crowd do to Jesus?
    a) They grab him to turn him over to the authorities.
    b) They shout "Hosanna!" and wave palm branches.
    c) They carry him on their shoulders and sing, "For He's a Jolly Good Fellow."

MEDITATION:

Jesus is very aware of the disciples' desire to obey him and please him. But he also understands their weak, human nature that conflicts with what their spiritual nature wants.

Think of some situations that you were in last week, where you wanted to obey Jesus and do the right thing, but for some reason you did not.

Ask Jesus to forgive you for your shortcomings last week.

Then ask him to remind you to ask for his strength when you encounter similar situations this week.

Maundy Thursday

First read the entire passage — Matthew 27:1–2, 11–26.

Now when morning had come, all the chief priests and the elders of the people took counsel against Jesus to put him to death: and they bound him, and led him away, and delivered him up to Pontius Pilate, the governor.

Now Jesus stood before the governor: and the governor asked him, saying, "Are you the King of the Jews?" Jesus said to him, "So you say." When he was accused by the chief priests and elders, he answered nothing. Then Pilate said to him, "Don't you hear how many things they testify against you? "He gave him no answer, not even one word, so that the governor marveled greatly.

Now at the feast the governor was accustomed to release to the multitude one prisoner, whom they desired. They had then a notable prisoner, called Barabbas. When therefore they were gathered together, Pilate said to them, "Whom do you want me to release to you? Barabbas, or Jesus, who is called Christ?" For he knew that because of envy they had delivered him up. While he was sitting on the judgment seat, his wife sent to him, saying, "Have nothing to do with that righteous man, for I have suffered many things today in a dream because of him."

Now the chief priests and the elders persuaded the multitudes to ask for Barabbas, and destroy Jesus. But the governor answered them, "Which of the two do you want me to release to you?" They said, "Barabbas!" Pilate said to them, "What then shall I do to Jesus, who is called Christ?" They all said to him, "Let him be crucified!" But the governor said, "Why? What evil has he done?" But they cried out exceedingly, saying, "Let him be crucified!"

So when Pilate saw that nothing was being gained, but rather that a disturbance was starting, he took water, and washed his hands before the multitude, saying, "I am innocent of the blood of this righteous person. You see to it." All the people answered, "May his blood be on us, and on our children!" Then he released to them Barabbas, but Jesus he flogged and delivered to be crucified.

Now re-read verses 1–2.

Now when morning had come, all the chief priests and the elders of the people took counsel against Jesus to put him to death: and they bound him, and led him away, and delivered him up to Pontius Pilate, the governor.

1. This is the morning after the crowd grabbed and arrested Jesus in the garden of Gethsemane. The chief priests and the other religious leaders are now scheming a plan for how they can get rid of Jesus. What is their plan?
   a) They plan to release him into the custody of his mother.
   b) They plan to send him to America.
   c) They plan to execute him.

2. Then they bind Jesus and take him to the Roman governor, since the Romans governed that land. What is the governor's name?
   a) Pontius Pilate
   b) Ben Hur
   c) Caiaphas

Now re-read verses 11–14.

Now Jesus stood before the governor: and the governor asked him, saying, "Are you the King of the Jews?" Jesus said to him, "So you say." When he was accused by the chief priests and elders, he answered nothing. Then Pilate said to him, "Don't you hear how many things they testify against you?" He gave him no answer, not even one word, so that the governor marveled greatly.

1. Now here we are at Jesus' trial. What does the governor ask Jesus?
   a) Are you hungry yet?
   b) Will You promise to stop healing sick people on the Sabbath?
   c) Are you the King of the Jews?

2. What is Jesus' answer to Pilate?
   a) You said it.
   b) I refuse to answer.
   c) Why do you want to know?

3. Then the chief priests and the other religious leaders accuse Jesus. How does he respond?
   a) He says nothing.
   b) He cries.
   c) He laughs at their accusations.

Now re-read verses 15–19

> Now at the feast the governor was accustomed to release to the multitude one prisoner, whom they desired. They had then a notable prisoner, called Barabbas. When therefore they were gathered together, Pilate said to them, "Whom do you want me to release to you? Barabbas, or Jesus, who is called Christ?" For he knew that because of envy they had delivered him up. While he was sitting on the judgment seat, his wife sent to him, saying, "Have nothing to do with that righteous man, for I have suffered many things today in a dream because of him."

1. The Jews are still celebrating the Passover Celebration. Every year, as part of the Passover Celebration, the Roman government releases one prisoner. They allow the Jewish people to select which prisoner they want freed. Pilate gives the crowd a choice between two prisoners. What are the names of these two prisoners?
   a) Barabbas and Jesus
   b) Al Capone and Billy Graham
   c) Goliath and King David

2. Someone dreamed about Jesus last night and tells Pilate to not be involved in any plan to harm Jesus. Who is this person?
   a) Pilate's mother.
   b) Pilate's wife.
   c) Caiaphas, the high priest.

3. What did Pilate's wife call Jesus?
   a) A crazy lunatic.
   b) A good cook.
   c) A righteous man.

Now re-read verses 20–23

> Now the chief priests and the elders persuaded the multitudes to ask for Barabbas, and destroy Jesus. But the governor answered them, "Which of the two do you want me to release to you?" They said, "Barabbas!" Pilate said to them, "What then shall I do to Jesus, who is called Christ?" They all said to him, "Let him be crucified!" But the governor said, "Why? What evil has he done?" But they cried out exceedingly, saying, "Let him be crucified!"

1. Which prisoner does the crowd choose to be released?
   a) Barabbas
   b) Jesus
   c) Jesse James

2. Why does the crowd select this person?
   a) The chief priests and the other religious leaders persuade them to do so.
   b) They always select the worst criminal.
   c) They always pick the guy with the shortest haircut.

3. Governor Pilate asks the crowd what they want him to do with Jesus. What do they shout?
   a) "Let him preach to us!"
   b) "Release him!"
   c) "Crucify him!"

Now re-read verses 24–26

> So when Pilate saw that nothing was being gained, but rather that a disturbance was starting, he took water, and washed his hands before the multitude, saying, "I am innocent of the blood of this righteous person. You see to it." All the people answered, "May his blood be on us, and on our children!" Then he released to them Barabbas, but Jesus he flogged and delivered to be crucified.

1. When Pilate washes his hands in front of the crowd, he is doing so not because his hands are dirty, but to symbolize something. What does he want to symbolize to the people?
   a) That he is innocent of Jesus' execution.
   b) That it's time to eat the Passover Feast.
   c) That Ivory soap is better than Irish Spring.

2. Which of these is closest to what the people shout after Pilate washes his hands?
   a) "We want a new governor!"
   b) "We'll blame you for Jesus' death as long as we live!"
   c) "We'll take the blame for Jesus' death!"

3. Pilate then releases Barabbas and gives orders for Jesus to be flogged and then crucified. Look up the word "flog" in your dictionary. What does it mean?
   a) To wash and prepare a person for surgery.
   b) To beat someone severely with a whip.
   c) To run bamboo under a person's fingernails.

4. What did Pilate call Jesus?
   a) A crazy lunatic.
   b) A talented carpenter.
   c) A righteous person.

MEDITATION:

The crowd asks for the release of Barabbas, a notorious criminal, even though they realize that Jesus is obviously innocent of a crime.

According to Mark 15:7 and Luke 23:19, Barabbas was a murderer who had been a part of an insurrection against the Roman government.

Perhaps they ask for the release of Barabbas because they understand him. They understand his desire for a violent overthrow of the Roman government. They don't understand why Jesus would want to be the Prince of Peace.

Barabbas' lifestyle could be described as:

- My way or the highway.

- Nobody's the boss of me.

- I don't care what happens to anyone else as long as I get my way.

Think of three ways to describe Jesus' lifestyle.

- _____.

- _____.

- _____.

Reflect on your own lifestyle and life choices. Do they match any of those described above?

GOOD FRIDAY

First read the entire passage — Matthew 27:32–50.

Today's Scripture passage takes place after the Roman soldiers tortured Jesus. As verse 32 begins, "they" refers to the Roman soldiers.

As they came out, they found a man of Cyrene, Simon by name, and they compelled him to go with them, that he might carry his cross. They came to a place called "Golgotha", that is to say, "The place of a skull."

They gave him sour wine to drink mixed with gall. When he had tasted it, he would not drink. When they had crucified him, they divided his clothing among them, casting lots, and they sat and watched him there. They set up over his head the accusation against him written, "THIS IS JESUS, THE KING OF THE JEWS."

Then there were two robbers crucified with him, one on his right hand and one on the left. Those who passed by blasphemed him, wagging their heads, and saying, "You who destroy the temple, and build it in three days, save yourself! If you are the Son of God, come down from the cross!" Likewise the chief priests also mocking, with the scribes, the Pharisees, and the elders, said, "He saved others, but he can't save himself. If he is the King of Israel, let him come down from the cross now, and we will believe in him. He trusts in God. Let God deliver him now, if he wants him; for he said, 'I am the Son of God.'" The robbers also who were crucified with him cast on him the same reproach.

Now from the sixth hour there was darkness over all the land until the ninth hour. About the ninth hour Jesus cried with a loud voice, saying, "Eli, Eli, lima sabachthani?" That is, "My God, my God, why have you forsaken me?" Some of them who stood there, when they heard it, said, "This man is calling Elijah." Immediately one of them ran, and took a sponge, and filled it with vinegar, and put it on a reed, and gave him a drink. The rest said, "Let him be. Let's see whether Elijah comes to save him." Jesus cried again with a loud voice, and yielded up his spirit.

Now re-read verses 32–33.

Here's some notes to help you understand verses 32–33 better:

In those days, those who were sentenced to be crucified had to carry their own cross to the place of crucifixion. However, since Jesus has been severely beaten and whipped, he does not have the strength to carry his cross.

In that region, the place where they crucified criminals was called "Golgotha."

As they came out, they found a man of Cyrene, Simon by name, and they compelled him to go with them, that he might carry his cross. They came to a place called "Golgotha", that is to say, "The place of a skull."

1. The Roman soldiers make an innocent bystander carry Jesus' cross. Who is this person?
   a) A man from Cyrene named Simon.
   b) A woman from Galilee named Mary.
   c) One of Jesus' disciples, Peter.

2. What does "Golgotha" mean in English?
   a) The garden beside a lake.
   b) The promised land.
   c) The place of the skull.

Now re-read verses 34–37

They gave him sour wine to drink mixed with gall. When he had tasted it, he would not drink. When they had crucified him, they divided his clothing among them, casting lots, and they sat and watched him there. They set up over his head the accusation against him written, "THIS IS JESUS, THE KING OF THE JEWS."

1. Since Jesus is in such pain, they offer him some wine mixed with a pain-killing drug called gall. What does Jesus do?
   a) He tastes it, and when he realizes it has gall in it, he refuses it.
   b) He tastes it, and when he realizes it has gall in it, he drinks it all.
   c) He asks them for some ice water instead.

2. They put a sign on the cross, above Jesus' head. It states his "crime" (the reason he is being crucified). What does the sign say?
   a) THIS IS JESUS, THE THIEF
   b) THIS IS JESUS, THE MURDERER
   c) THIS IS JESUS, THE KING OF THE JEWS

Now re-read verses 38–44.

Here's some notes to help you understand verses 38–44 better:

Two other men are also crucified — one on Jesus' right and one on his left. Crucifixion was the penalty for treason and crimes against the Roman government.

In verse 38, the World English Bible translates the original Greek word *lestes* as *robber*. This same Greek word is often translated as *rebel*, referring to a revolutionary.

Then there were two robbers crucified with him, one on his right hand and one on the left. Those who passed by blasphemed him, wagging their heads, and saying, "You who destroy the temple, and build it in three days, save yourself! If you are the Son of God, come down from the cross!" Likewise the chief priests also mocking, with the scribes, the Pharisees, and the elders, said, "He saved others, but he can't save himself. If he is the King of Israel, let him come down from the cross now, and we will believe in him. He trusts in God. Let God deliver him now, if he wants him; for he said, 'I am the Son of God.'" The robbers also who were crucified with him cast on him the same reproach.

1. There are two men who are also crucified with Jesus. Who do you think these two men rebelled against?
   a) Their parents.
   b) Their boss.
   c) The Roman government.

2. The people are mocking Jesus while he is suffering on the cross. What do they say?
   a) If You're really the Son of God, preach to us now.
   b) If You're really the Son of God, come down from the cross.
   c) If You're really the Son of God, turn these rocks into bread.

3. The chief priests and the other religious leaders also mock Jesus. What do they say?
   a) Come down from the cross and we'll crucify someone of your choice in your place.
   b) Come down from the cross and we'll let you go to jail instead.
   c) Come down from the cross and we'll believe in You.

Now re-read verses 45–50.

Now from the sixth hour there was darkness over all the land until the ninth hour. About the ninth hour Jesus cried with a loud voice, saying, "Eli, Eli, lima sabachthani?" That is, "My God, my God, why have you forsaken me?" Some of them who stood there, when they heard it, said, "This man is calling Elijah." Immediately one of them ran, and took a sponge, and filled it with vinegar, and put it on a reed, and gave him a drink. The rest said, "Let him be. Let's see whether Elijah comes to save him." Jesus cried again with a loud voice, and yielded up his spirit.

1. The first hour of the day is 6:00 a.m. What time is the sixth hour??
   a) 12:00 noon.
   b) 2:30 p.m.
   c) 7:00 a.m.

2. What happened between noon and 3:00 p.m. that day?
   a) A tornado wiped out the country.
   b) The sky turned as dark as night.
   c) It rained so hard that the whole land flooded.

MEDITATION:

The chief priests and the other religious leaders mock Jesus while he's on the cross by saying, "Let him come down from the cross now, and we will believe in him."

They don't understand that if Jesus did come down from the cross, he would defeat God's purpose.

If he had performed a miracle by coming down from the cross, it is possible that the crowd who were mocking him may have believed that he was the Son of God. But thanks be to God — he stayed to the point of death so that billions of people for all generations to come might believe in him and be forgiven of their sins.

Take sixty seconds to close your eyes and try to imagine the scene at Golgotha. Use your imagination's five senses:

- Try to see Jesus on the cross, even though darkness is covering the land during the last hours of his life.

- Touch the rough wood of Jesus' cross.

- Taste the dust that's been kicked up by all the people who pass by and are mocking him.

- Hear Jesus try to breathe.

- Smell the death in the air.

Holy Saturday

First read the entire passage — Matthew 27:55–66.

Many women were there watching from afar, who had followed Jesus from Galilee, serving him. Among them were Mary Magdalene, Mary the mother of James and Joses, and the mother of the sons of Zebedee. When evening had come, a rich man from Arimathaea, named Joseph, who himself was also Jesus' disciple came. This man went to Pilate, and asked for Jesus' body. Then Pilate commanded the body to be given up.

Joseph took the body, and wrapped it in a clean linen cloth, and laid it in his own new tomb, which he had cut out in the rock, and he rolled a great stone to the door of the tomb, and departed. Mary Magdalene was there, and the other Mary, sitting opposite the tomb.

Now on the next day, which was the day after the Preparation Day, the chief priests and the Pharisees were gathered together to Pilate, saying, "Sir, we remember what that deceiver said while he was still alive: 'After three days I will rise again.' Command therefore that the tomb be made secure until the third day, lest perhaps his disciples come at night and steal him away, and tell the people, 'He is risen from the dead;' and the last deception will be worse than the first." Pilate said to them, "You have a guard. Go, make it as secure as you can." So they went with the guard and made the tomb secure, sealing the stone.

Now re-read verses 55–58.

Many women were there watching from afar, who had followed Jesus from Galilee, serving him. Among them were Mary Magdalene, Mary the mother of James and Joses, and the mother of the sons of Zebedee. When evening had come, a rich man from Arimathaea, named Joseph, who himself was also Jesus' disciple came. This man went to Pilate, and asked for Jesus' body. Then Pilate commanded the body to be given up.

1. Many women who were followers of Jesus watched his crucifixion. Matthew specifically mentions three women who were there. Note that Matthew does not mention Mary, the mother of Jesus by name — perhaps he thought it was obvious that she was there. Which three women does Matthew specifically mention?
   a) Ruth, Naomi, and Orpah.
   b) Mary (the mother of James and Joseph), Zebedee's wife, and Mary Magdalene.
   c) Corrie ten Boom, Susanna Wesley, and Mother Teresa.

2. One of Jesus' followers is a rich man from Arimathea. What is his name?
   a) Joseph
   b) Nicodemus
   c) Simeon

3. This man from Arimathea goes to Pilate to ask him for something. What does he want?
   a) The cross Jesus died on.
   b) The sign they nailed on the cross, above Jesus' head.
   c) Jesus' body.

Now re-read verses 59–61.

Joseph took the body, and wrapped it in a clean linen cloth, and laid it in his own new tomb, which he had cut out in the rock, and he rolled a great stone to the door of the tomb, and departed. Mary Magdalene was there, and the other Mary, sitting opposite the tomb.

1. What does Joseph do with the body of Jesus when Pilate allows him to have it?
   a) He takes it to the temple in Arimathea.
   b) He wraps it in a clean linen cloth that they use when they bury people.
   c) He delivers it to Mary, Jesus' mother.

2. Joseph of Arimathea puts Jesus' body in a new, never-been-used tomb. This is the tomb that Joseph had bought for himself. What does he put in the doorway of the tomb after he lays Jesus' body in the tomb?
   a) A large stone.
   b) A memorial plaque.
   c) A wreath.

Now re-read verses 62–66.

> Now on the next day, which was the day after the Preparation Day, the chief priests and the Pharisees were gathered together to Pilate, saying, "Sir, we remember what that deceiver said while he was still alive: 'After three days I will rise again.' Command therefore that the tomb be made secure until the third day, lest perhaps his disciples come at night and steal him away, and tell the people, 'He is risen from the dead;' and the last deception will be worse than the first." Pilate said to them, "You have a guard. Go, make it as secure as you can." So they went with the guard and made the tomb secure, sealing the stone.

1. Now it is the day after Jesus died. Governor Pilate has some visitors. Who are they?
   a) The twelve disciples.
   b) Mary and Joseph, the parents of Jesus.
   c) The chief priests and the Pharisees.

2. What do they want Pilate to do?
   a) Make sure that Jesus' disciples do not steal his body.
   b) Release another prisoner.
   c) Arrest Barabbas again and crucify him.

3. Why do they want Pilate to do this?
   a) Because this is customary during the Passover Celebration.
   b) Because they're afraid the disciples will make it look like Jesus rose from the dead.
   c) Because they want to overthrow the Roman government.

4. What does Pilate do for them?
   a) He appoints a Jew to be the assistant governor.
   b) He gives them permission to seal the tomb and gives them some soldiers to guard it.
   c) He orders some soldiers to move Jesus' body to another tomb.

MEDITATION:

Joseph of Arimathea takes a big risk when he asks for the body of Jesus. Jesus had been condemned of treason and Pilate might have arrested Joseph for supporting Jesus. Joseph didn't know at that time that Jesus would be raised from the dead.

What risks do you take for your faith in Jesus?

For example — do you behave like a Christian when such behavior may be unpopular?

Think of a specific occasion when this happened.

Easter Sunday

First read the entire passage — Matthew 28:1–10.

Now after the Sabbath, as it began to dawn on the first day of the week, Mary Magdalene and the other Mary came to see the tomb. Behold, there was a great earthquake, for an angel of the Lord descended from the sky, and came and rolled away the stone from the door, and sat on it. His appearance was like lightning, and his clothing white as snow. For fear of him, the guards shook, and became like dead men.

The angel answered the women, "Don't be afraid, for I know that you seek Jesus, who has been crucified. He is not here, for he has risen, just like he said. Come, see the place where the Lord was lying. Go quickly and tell his disciples, 'He has risen from the dead, and behold, he goes before you into Galilee; there you will see him.' Behold, I have told you."

They departed quickly from the tomb with fear and great joy, and ran to bring his disciples word. As they went to tell his disciples, behold, Jesus met them, saying, "Rejoice!" They came and took hold of his feet, and worshiped him. Then Jesus said to them, "Don't be afraid. Go tell my brothers that they should go into Galilee, and there they will see me."

Now re-read verses 1–4.

Now after the Sabbath, as it began to dawn on the first day of the week, Mary Magdalene and the other Mary came to see the tomb. Behold, there was a great earthquake, for an angel of the Lord descended from the sky, and came and rolled away the stone from the door, and sat on it. His appearance was like lightning, and his clothing white as snow. For fear of him, the guards shook, and became like dead men.

1. What happens?
    a) A tornado hits.
    b) An earthquake hits.
    c) It snows.

2. What causes this to happen?
    a) An angel rolls away the rock that sealed the tomb.
    b) A volcano erupted.
    c) No one knows.

3. Who is wearing dazzling white clothes and has a face that shines like lightening?
    a) Governor Pontius Pilate
    b) Luke Skywalker
    c) The angel of the Lord

4. What happens to the soldiers that are guarding the tomb when they see this person?
    a) They all shake with fear and then fall into a dead faint.
    b) They shout "Hosanna!" and start to dance.
    c) They run away in different directions.

Now re-read verses 5–7.

> The angel answered the women, "Don't be afraid, for I know that you seek Jesus, who has been crucified. He is not here, for he has risen, just like he said. Come, see the place where the Lord was lying. Go quickly and tell his disciples, 'He has risen from the dead, and behold, he goes before you into Galilee; there you will see him.' Behold, I have told you."

1. The angel tells the two women that Jesus is not here. Why isn't his body here? What has happened?
    a) Jesus has risen, just like he said he would.
    b) Jesus has risen, much to God's surprise.
    c) Jesus' body has been moved to another tomb.

2. The angel tells them to do two things. What is the first thing?
   a) Roll the rock back where it was so the guards won't get mad.
   b) Put some perfume and spices on Jesus' body.
   c) Look in the tomb and see for yourselves that Jesus' body isn't there anymore.

3. What is the second thing the angel tells them to do?
   a) Run and tell the disciples that Jesus has risen from the dead.
   b) If it comes up in conversation, tell your friends that Jesus has risen from the dead.
   c) Whatever you do, keep your mouth shut about what you've seen.

4. What's going to happen in Galilee?
   a) The disciples are going to have a memorial service for Jesus there.
   b) Jesus will be there and spend some time with them.
   c) The play, "Cotton Patch Gospel," will be playing there for three nights only.

Now re-read verses 8–10.

> They departed quickly from the tomb with fear and great joy, and ran to bring his disciples word. As they went to tell his disciples, behold, Jesus met them, saying, "Rejoice!" They came and took hold of his feet, and worshiped him. Then Jesus said to them, "Don't be afraid. Go tell my brothers that they should go into Galilee, and there they will see me."

1. What do the two Marys do?
   a) They run to tell the disciples what has happened.
   b) They shake with fear and fall into a dead faint.
   c) They pour the perfume and spices on the angel.

2. Who talks to them on the way home?
   a) Some of Pilate's soldiers.
   b) Peter and John.
   c) Jesus.

3. What do the two Marys do when they see him?
   a) They run back to the tomb and look for the angel.
   b) They fall to the ground and worship him.
   c) They ignore him.

4. What does he tell them to do?
   a) Tell my followers to convert to Hinduism.
   b) Tell my followers to escape from this country while they still can.
   c) Tell my followers to meet me in Galilee.

MEDITATION:

The two Marys come to the tomb in order to prepare Jesus' body for burial. They do this because they loved Jesus and they want to give honor to his dead body. They are very surprised when the angel tells them that Jesus has risen from the dead.

The two Marys were faithful to Jesus, even when they thought he was dead. We should be even more faithful to Jesus because we know that he is alive and with us today.

Think of one specific thing that you can do for Jesus today.

EASTER MONDAY

First read the entire passage — Matthew 28:11–20.

Today's Scripture passage takes place after Jesus appears to the two Marys. As verse 11 begins, "they" refers to the two Marys, running to tell the disciples that Jesus wants them to meet him in Galilee.

Now while they were going, behold, some of the guards came into the city, and told the chief priests all the things that had happened. When they were assembled with the elders, and had taken counsel, they gave a large amount of silver to the soldiers, saying, "Say that his disciples came by night, and stole him away while we slept. If this comes to the governor's ears, we will persuade him and make you free of worry." So they took the money and did as they were told. This saying was spread abroad among the Jews, and continues until today.

But the eleven disciples went into Galilee, to the mountain where Jesus had sent them. When they saw him, they bowed down to him, but some doubted.

Jesus came to them and spoke to them, saying, "All authority has been given to me in heaven and on earth. Go and make disciples of all nations, baptizing them in the name of the Father and of the Son and of the Holy Spirit, teaching them to observe all things that I commanded you. Behold, I am with you always, even to the end of the age." Amen.

Now re-read verse 11–15.

Now while they were going, behold, some of the guards came into the city, and told the chief priests all the things that had happened.

When they were assembled with the elders, and had taken counsel, they gave a large amount of silver to the soldiers, saying, "Say that his disciples came by night, and stole him away while we slept. If this comes to the governor's ears, we will persuade him and make you free of worry." So they took the money and did as they were told. This saying was spread abroad among the Jews, and continues until today.

1. While the two Marys are on their way to tell the disciples about Jesus, the soldiers that were guarding the tomb go into the city. Who do the soldiers talk to about what happened at the tomb?
   a) Pontius Pilate and Herod.
   b) The twelve disciples.
   c) The chief priests.

2. The religious leaders have an emergency meeting. What is their plan of action?
   a) They pay the soldiers "hush money" to lie about what happened at the tomb.
   b) They ask the soldiers to tell everyone that Jesus has risen from the dead.
   c) They plan to meet Jesus in Galilee so they can ask him to help them overthrow the Roman government.

3. What are the soldiers supposed to say to the people?
   a) Jesus' disciples stole his body last night while we were asleep.
   b) Jesus wasn't really dead. He was in a coma. He woke up and walked out of his tomb.
   c) We secretly put Jesus' body in another tomb, and now we can't remember where it is.

Now re-read verses 16–17.

But the eleven disciples went into Galilee, to the mountain where Jesus had sent them. When they saw him, they bowed down to him, but some doubted.

1. Where do the disciples go?
   a) Bethlehem
   b) Garden of Gethsemane
   c) Galilee

2. Why do they go there?
   a) That's where they go every day to pray.
   b) The fish are biting there this time of year.
   c) Jesus said he'd meet them there.

3. Matthew tells us that only eleven of the twelve disciples go there. Who do you think the missing disciple is? (If you need help, look up Matthew 27:3–5.)
   a) Peter
   b) Judas Iscariot
   c) Philip

Now re-read verses 18–20

> Jesus came to them and spoke to them, saying, "All authority has been given to me in heaven and on earth. Go and make disciples of all nations, baptizing them in the name of the Father and of the Son and of the Holy Spirit, teaching them to observe all things that I commanded you. Behold, I am with you always, even to the end of the age." Amen.

1. Jesus tells them that he has been given all authority in heaven and on earth. What does he tell them to do?
   a) Try to forget that you ever knew me.
   b) Go all over the world and help other people decide to become my disciples.
   c) Wash behind your ears and brush your teeth every night.

2. What else does Jesus tell them to do?
   a) Train all new disciples to overthrow the Roman government.
   b) Feed and clothe all new disciples.
   c) Baptize all new disciples and teach them to obey all my commands.

3. What's the last thing Jesus tells them?
   a) I am with you Monday through Friday during regular business hours, even to the end of the age.
   b) I am with you on Sundays when you're in church, even to the end of the age.
   c) I am with you always, even to the end of the age.

MEDITATION:

There are still people who do not believe that Jesus has risen from the dead. Here are some of the reasons they give for not believing:

- Some people say that Jesus' resurrection was only a legend and it didn't really happen.

- Others say that Jesus wasn't really dead, so he couldn't be raised from the dead if he wasn't dead in the first place.

- Others say that the disciples must have hidden Jesus' body.

But people who believe in Jesus know that he was raised from the dead, because they have experienced him in their lives.

If someone asked you why you believe Jesus is alive today, how would you answer?

Think of two reasons why you believe Jesus is alive today.

Did you enjoy working through this Bible study as much as I enjoyed writing it?

Your feedback is invaluable to me and to future readers.

I hope you'll consider leaving a review on Amazon.

Thanks in advance for your support!

~ Celesta

Answers

PALM SUNDAY

Verses 1–3

1b. Jesus and his disciples were outside of a village called Bethsphage, which is on the eastern slope of the Mount of Olives. Bethsphage is about a half mile from Jerusalem.

2a. Jesus sends two of his disciples on an errand.

3b. Jesus sends them into the village of Bethsphage.

4b. Jesus tell them they'll find a donkey and her colt.

5c. The disciples are to say that "The Lord needs them."

Verses 4–5

1a Jesus told them to bring back a donkey and her colt so that he could fulfill the Zechariah's prophecy as the Messiah.

2b. According to Zechariah's prophecy, the humble King arrives, riding on a donkey.

3a. Jesus is the king that fulfills the prophecy in Zechariah 9:9.

Verses 6–11

1a. A large crowd spread their clothes on the road and others cut branches from the trees and spread them on the road.

2b. The crowd shouted, "Hosanna to the son of David! Blessed is he who comes in the name of the Lord! Hosanna in the highest!"

Verses 12–14

1a. Jesus has just entered the temple of God.

2b. Jesus drove out all of those who sold and bought in the temple because God's house is a house of prayer.

3c. When the blind and the lame came to Jesus in the temple, he healed them.

Answers

HOLY MONDAY

Verses 1–2

1a. Jesus is talking to his disciples.

2c. Jesus says that Passover is coming up in two days.

3a. Jesus tells his disciples that the Son of Man will be crucified during Passover.

4a. Jesus is the Son of Man.

Verses 3–5

1a. The high priest, chief priests, scribes, and elders took counsel together that they might take Jesus and kill him.

2b. The chief priests, scribes, and elders gathered together in the court of the high priest, who was called Caiaphas.

3b. They plan to wait until after the Passover feast, lest a riot occur among the people. However, the timing of their plan was changed when Judas betrayed Jesus.

Verses 6–13

1c. A lady pours expensive ointment on Jesus' head as he sat at the table of Simon the leper.

2b. The disciples were upset because this was very expensive ointment that could have been sold in order to help the poor.

3b. Jesus answers his disciples that this woman has done a good work for him.

4c. Jesus tells his disciples that when the woman poured the expensive ointment on him, it symbolized preparing his body for burial.

Verses 14–16

1a. Judas Iscariot meets with the chief priests.

2c. Judas asks the chief priests how much they'll pay him if he delivers Jesus into their hands. They pay him thirty pieces of silver.

HOLY TUESDAY

Verses 17–22

1b. The disciples ask Jesus where he wants to eat the Passover.

2c. Jesus celebrated the Passover meal with the twelve disciples.

3a. The disciples were exceedingly sorrowful when Jesus told them that one of them would betray him.

4c. Each disciple began to ask him, "It isn't me, is it, Lord?"

Verses 23–25

1c. Jesus says his betrayer would be better off if he had not been born.

2b. When Judas asks Jesus, "It isn't me, is it, Rabbi," Jesus answers him, "You said it."

Verse 26

1c. Jesus took bread, gave thanks for it, and broke it. Some translations use the phrase "blessed it" in place of "gave thanks for it." It was customary to say a blessing of thanksgiving over the bread at mealtime.

2a. When Jesus broke the bread and gave it to his disciples, he said, "Take, eat; this is my body."

Verses 27–30

1b. Jesus took the cup and gave thanks.

2a. When Jesus gave them the cup, he said, "This is my blood of the new covenant."

3b. Jesus tells them that his blood is poured out for many for the remission of sins.

4a. When they had sung a hymn, they went out to the Mount of Olives.

SPY WEDNESDAY

Verses 36–38

1c. Jesus came with his disciples to Gethsemane.

2b. Jesus takes Peter and the two sons of Zebedee with him.

3a. Jesus tells them that his soul is exceedingly sorrowful.

4c. Jesus tells them to stay and keep watch with him.

Verse 39

1b. Jesus asks God the Father to take this cup from him.

2c. The cup Jesus speaks of signifies the suffering he is about to endure.

3a. Jesus ends this prayer to God the Father: "nevertheless, not what I desire, but what you desire."

Verses 40–41

1c. The three disciples (Peter and the two sons of Zebedee) are sleeping.

2a. Though the Scripture does not tell us how Jesus felt when he found the three disciples asleep, his tone seems as if he's disappointed in them — "What, couldn't you watch with me for one hour?"

3c. Jesus tells them to stay awake and pray so that they don't enter into temptation.

4a. "The spirit is willing, but the flesh is weak" means that though we have good intentions, it's difficult for us to follow through with them.

Verses 42–46

1a. Jesus prays three times in the Garden of Gethsemane.

2c. It is time for the Son of Man to be betrayed.

Verses 47–50

1a. Judas came with a crowd of people with swords and clubs.

2b. Judas kisses Jesus to give the crowd a signal of who they should grab.

3a. They laid hands on Jesus and took him.

MAUNDY THURSDAY

Verses 1–2

1c. All the chief priests and the elders of the people took counsel against Jesus to put him to death.

2a. The Roman governor's name is Pontius Pilate.

Verses 11–14

1c. The governor asked Jesus, "Are you the King of the Jews?"

2a. Jesus answered the governor, "So you say."

3a. When Jesus was accused by the chief priests and elders, he answered nothing.

Verses 15–19

1a. Governor Pilate asks the crowd whom they want him to release to them — Barabbas or Jesus.

2b. Governor Pilate's wife warns him to not have anything to do with Jesus because she had a bad dream about him.

3c. Pilate's wife referred to Jesus as a righteous man.

Verses 20–23

1a. When Pilate asks the crowd whom they want to have released to them, they shout, "Barabbas!"

2a. The chief priests and the elders persuaded the crowd to ask for Barabbas and destroy Jesus.

3c. When Pilate asks the crowd what he should do to Jesus, they shout, "Let him be crucified!"

Verses 24–26

1a. Pilate said, "I am innocent of the blood of this righteous person."

2c. The people shout that they'll take the blame for Jesus' death for generations to come.

3b. To flog someone is to beat them with a whip or rod.

4c. Pilate called Jesus a righteous person.

GOOD FRIDAY

Verses 32–33

1a. The Roman soldiers found a man of Cyrene named Simon, and they made him go with them that he might carry Jesus' cross.

2c. Golgotha means "The place of a skull."

Verses 34–37

1a. When Jesus had tasted it, he would not drink.

2c. They set a sign on the cross over Jesus' head that read, "THIS IS JESUS, THE KING OF THE JEWS."

Verses 38–44

1c. The two men who were crucified with Jesus are described as "robbers." The Greek word used here is often translated as "rebel," referring to someone who is a revolutionary against the government. Most likely, they were arrested for acts of rebellion against the Roman government.

2b. Those who passed by blasphemed Jesus, saying, "If you are the Son of God, come down from the cross!"

3c. The chief priests, the scribes, the Pharisees, and the elders said, "If he is the King of Israel, let him come down from the cross now, and we will believe in him."

Verses 45–50

1a. The sixth hour of the day is the beginning of the middle of the day, which is twelve o'clock noon.

2b. All the land was covered in darkness, which lasted between the sixth hour (noon) until the ninth hour (3 p.m.).

HOLY SATURDAY

Verses 55–58

1b. Among the women who were watching the crucifixion from afar were Mary Magdalene, Mary the mother of James and Joses, and the mother of the sons of Zebedee.

2a. Joseph of Arimathea was a rich man who was a disciple of Jesus.

3c. Joseph of Arimathea asked Pilate for Jesus' body.

Verses 59–61

1b. Joseph of Arimathea took the body of Jesus and wrapped it in a clean linen cloth and laid it in his own new tomb.

2a. Joseph of Arimathea rolled a great stone to the door of the tomb.

Verses 62–66

1c. On the next day, the chief priests and the Pharisees gathered together to Pilate.

2a. The chief priests and the Pharisees asked Pilate to command that the tomb be made secure, so that Jesus' disciples could not come at night and steal his body.

3b. They are concerned that Jesus' disciples will steal his body and then tell the people that Jesus rose from the dead.

4b. Pilate gives them a guard and permission to make the tomb as secure as they can.

EASTER SUNDAY

Verses 1–4

1b. There was a great earthquake.

2a. An angel of the Lord descended from the sky and came and rolled away the stone from the door of the tomb.

3c. An angel of the Lord had an appearance like lightning, and his clothing was white as snow.

4a. The guards shook and became like dead men.

Verses 5–7

1a. Jesus is not in the tomb, for he has risen, just like he said.

2c. First, the angel tells the women to go in the tomb and see the place where the body of Jesus was lying.

3a. The angel tells the women to go quickly and tell his disciples that Jesus has risen from the dead and that they are to meet him in Galilee.

4b. The disciples will see Jesus in Galilee.

Verses 8–10

1a. The two Marys ran to bring his disciples word.

2c. Jesus met the two Marys as they were running to tell the disciples.

3b. When Jesus appeared to the two Marys, they took hold of his feet and worshiped him.

4c. Jesus tells the two Marys to give a message to his followers that he will meet them in Galilee.

EASTER MONDAY

Verse 11–15

1c. Some of the guards told the chief priests all the things that had happened.

2a. The chief priests and the elders gave a large amount of silver to the soldiers and instructed them to lie about what happened.

3a. The chief priests and the elders paid the guards to say that Jesus' disciples came in the night and stole his body while they were sleeping.

Verses 16–17

1c. The eleven disciples went into Galilee.

2c. Jesus had sent the disciples to the mountain in Galilee.

3b. Judas Iscariot did not go with the disciples to meet the risen Christ in Galilee.

Verses 18–20

1b. Jesus tells his disciples to go and make disciples of all nations.

2c. Jesus tells his disciples to baptize new disciples in the name of the Father and of the Son and of the Holy Spirit, and to also teach them to observe all the things he has commanded them.

3c. Jesus tells his disciples that he is with us always, even to the end of the age.

JOIN THE TEAM

You can help improve the *Choose This Day Multiple Choice Bible Study Series* by sending your **comments** to www.fermatahouse.com/contact/.

And you can help make the Series more accessible to others by leaving a **review** on amazon.com. Amazon's search engine has an algorithm for visibility which is largely based on the number of **reviews** a book receives. Just a few words will suffice.

Thanks in advance!

MORE MULTIPLE CHOICE BIBLE STUDIES

Get ready for Christmas with the original source of the Christmas story – the Bible.

Like an Advent calendar, Getting Ready for Christmas begins on December 1 and ends December 25. Each day's Scripture passages are included (World English Bible) and point to Christ as the reason for the season.

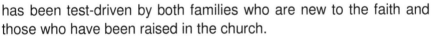

The entertaining multiple choice answers make this a fun Advent activity for the whole family and the short meditative questions can serve as discussion starters at the dinner table.

This Advent devotional book has been test-driven by both families who are new to the faith and those who have been raised in the church.

The month of December is busy and hectic as we check through our "Get Ready for Christmas" lists: Bake cookies. Address cards. Decorate the tree. Wrap gifts. Is getting our hearts ready on your list?

Use this book personally during a coffee break or with the family in the car or at the breakfast table to prepare for Christmas.

Getting Ready for Christmas:
25 Multiple Choice Bible Studies for Advent.

Available now at Amazon.com.

ALSO FROM FERMATA HOUSE...

Soldiers whose wounds glowed in the dark. A volunteer nurse whose orders even General Sherman followed. A woman who, when kidnapped by Confederate pirates, captured her captors. A slave who served as a U.S. congressman. A family who was "stalked" by the Civil War. Civilians running for their lives, picnic baskets flying. The memo Abraham Lincoln wrote, mentioning a saucy woman.

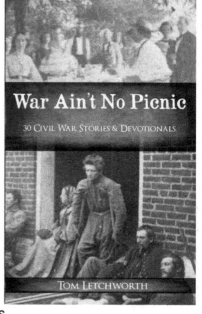

These are some of the interesting stories Tom Letchworth discovered in his research of the American Civil War. And since he's a United Methodist minister, it's only natural that he saw the spiritual analogies.

Each chapter contains historical photos and footnoted primary sources.

"These stories from the Civil War focus on little known events and people that prove grace can be found in the worst of circumstances."

"I loved the little stories about the Civil War! Also, loved how the devotionals went along with the stories!"

"This book is exactly what its title suggests: a collection of stories from the war, each one folded into a devotion and closed with an appropriate prayer. I enjoyed the book, and I think anyone with an interest in Civil-War studies would enjoy it also."

"Easy read with a correlation lesson from the Holy Scriptures at the end of each chapter."

"The writer has an engaging conversational style ... I have purchased several copies as gifts."

War Ain't No Picnic: 30 Civil War Stories & Devotionals.

Available now at Amazon.com.